Hey Helen!
Love your soul! I
appreciate your thirs~
and development. The
just being your

—your friend
Austin Zulauf

Austin Zulauf

ACTING CLASSES

ACTING CLASSES

DESIGN YOUR DREAM-SELF...
ATTRACT YOUR DREAM LIFE!

AUSTIN ZULAUF

NEXT CENTURY
PUBLISHING

ACTING CLASSES

Published by Next Century Publishing
Austin, TX
www.NextCenturyPublishing.com

ISBN: 978-1-68102-970-2
Library of Congress Control Number: 2017913983

Printed in the United States of America

Design your dream-self and attract your dream life!

A fun and easy way to become the best version of yourself possible…

AND attract limitless riches in 6 simple steps

I have to start by thanking my mother and father for helping me learn how to be a quality person with good integrity. From early on, they instilled in me the value of helping others while setting a good example. I can never repay you for all you have done for me, but I will continue to strive to live up to your example as a parent myself.

Thanks also to the many mentors that I have had over the years in both my professional career and my personal life, including some that I did not have the honor to meet personally. There are far too many to mention here, but I attribute a lot of my success and my spirit to W. Clement Stone's teachings and many other leaders from the Napoleon Hill Foundation. In addition, the guidance of John Whitaker, my first District Sales Manager when I worked for Combined Insurance Company, was priceless. I will be forever grateful to him. John always helped me learn the process that leads to success and enjoy the journey.

Last but not least, a special thanks to Peter Leighton for believing in me and giving me a shot because sometimes, that's all you need to change everything…just one shot!

TABLE OF CONTENTS

Introduction 1

I have traveled a long journey to get to where I am today – from rags to riches to rags and back again. Here's a look at the first steps on my journey – and why my greatest satisfaction in life is helping others to make the most of their own potential.

**Chapter 1: Decide what life you want.
(Do you even know what life you want?)** 21

What title would you like to have, what cars would you like to own? What is your life's mission? What spouse would make you happiest, what kind of friends would you like to surround yourself with…and perhaps most importantly, how do you think possessing these things would make you feel?

**Chapter 2: Do your research and find your
modeling mentors** 37

This is the step in which you research people who have the kind of life you want. This is important so that you can start observing them and modeling yourself after them. Research how they became the person they are today – their back story, what they do in their spare time, and how they came to shape their views on the world. The more detail you learn about their personal stories and the more you find out about what makes these people tick, the better.

Chapter 3: VISUALIZE! Don't think it is, KNOW it is! 45

Don't THINK you are, KNOW you are…get as detailed as possible with your visualization techniques. For example, how does your dream house smell? What does the leather in your car feel like, what's on the radio of that car? What color suits are you wearing? We'll do a cool visualization exercise in this chapter as well.

Chapter 4: Model, mirror & mimic (If it works for one man, it'll work for another) 55

There is nothing wrong at all with being a copycat – as long as you copy the right cat! Mimic their voice inflection, how they walk, their mannerisms, even phrases they use…check out their social media, what do they post about? When handling a situation, think about how THEY would handle it. Allow yourself to slip into their mindset.

Chapter 5: Create your character! (Slip into your role). 61

This gets FUN! Imagine that you are writing a role for a movie. Create a detailed design of the character in life that you'd like to be. Dress, think, act and BE the person you want to be in every way. Heck, it couldn't hurt to give your character some sort of name you can keep to remind yourself of who you're striving to be! In this chapter, you are actually writing the guidelines for an entire character and describing a person based off of the lessons in the first several chapters. You are just refining the person you would like to be – the very BEST version of YOU.

Chapter 6: Fail to succeed! (Begin your transition with the knowledge that success is often a series of corrected failures) 69

Don't get discouraged when you have a failure or a setback along the way. Winners don't have time for that junk! But if you DO become discouraged, remember your character and how THEY would handle it. When challenges or issues come up, that's fine! Learn from overcoming your failures &

issues. But really, it is only a failure if you accept it as such. There will inevitably be bumps in the road when on the path to achieving greatness. You not only have to persevere, you need to GET EXCITED when issues arise because you know all the average people would give up. You, on the other hand, speed up and greet challenges with a smile because you know that you will overcome!

Chapter 7: Dare to succeed – a few closing thoughts 79

Now that we have covered all of the basics on creating your ideal role, let's recap a few last thoughts on how to achieve real satisfaction and success.

ACTING
CLASSES

INTRODUCTION

I'm excited for you – because you are about to embark on an amazing journey.

As you absorb these pages, understand that you absolutely will not be the same person once you get done with this reading – and that is precisely the point.

You will, however, be closer to the very best version of yourself that you possibly can be. You will be seeing many times more happiness and progress toward your ultimate goals in life. And by the way, you'll be forced to develop much higher goals than you have right now and you will actually WANT to do so. More importantly than that, you'll actually achieve those goals!

You will essentially be tricked into using parts of your mind in a way you may not be familiar with. You will begin to design a "role" – a character that is the person you have always dreamed of becoming. Think of it as the very best version of you that exists on the highest plane of personal evolution within yourself…then you will become that person and attract your new dream life.

All of these things are for certain. I put an emphasis on "new" dream life because you just simply will not think the same as you progress through these simple steps laid out in these pages. You will become a person who dares to dream even higher than you already do. This metamorphosis is more than possible, it's more than likely, and it will be so dramatic that you'll end up looking back feeling like you've achieved what you previously believed was the impossible.

You may not even recognize your life at the end. You may feel like you've evolved and had a breakthrough to become someone who resonates such positive energy you lift others up just by being around them. You will attract a life beyond what you're currently able to dream – but it's not all a free ride.

You will need to do plenty of work of your own along the way. You will need to digest every page of this book well and put it to good use with good note taking, a high belief level and thorough follow-through. You don't need any particular gadget or tool to build a successful business – many of those are simply distractions. The barriers to entry are much lower than you think and all you really need is in your behavior and way of thinking. All you need is to bring focus to your daily activities and to hold yourself accountable to fulfilling the goals that you have set for yourself.

You may be thinking to yourself that this seems like quite a tall order – and you're right! This is no coloring book. Each chapter will lay out the fundamental concepts behind each step in my process, highlight some lessons I learned through experience on my journey along the way, and provide a few easy to implement, actionable steps that you can begin to do today.

But let's have some fun while we do it! I have learned that life is too short to take yourself too seriously. You will see as you progress through these steps that it's not only going to happen, you'll not only mold yourself and the world around you, you'll not only attract all of the personal and professional riches you desire into your life, but you will also have a sensational time doing so!

These steps will make the journey fun. So enjoy, take good notes and absorb these pages as if you know for certain all of your wildest dreams are waiting for you at the end of this book...because they're not much further IF you apply these steps thoroughly. Enjoy!

LESSONS FROM MY JOURNEY

This book is about you. It's about your future and where you are headed. But I want to first give you some context about my story and the journey I've taken to get to where I am today.

I'm proud that today I have created my own character and been able to live as my dream-self . I was fortunate enough to be trained by some of the top personal self-development gurus, top sales people and thought leaders in the world. My career and my life has truly been a blessing.

Today I have achieved much more than I could have imagined starting out. To name just a few of the things that I am most proud of:

- I've been a #1 income earner in not just one, not two, but three companies.
- I've built a team of more than 34,000 internationally – in just one year.
- I've been called upon as an outside sales consultant to major Fortune 500 corporations.

- I've been sought after for training and success systems and trainings that help families grow together.

- My training has helped more than 370 families (and counting) around the world retire from the full-time grind of work and pursue their greatest passions in life.

- I've achieved financial independence that allows me to work when I want to because I am passionate about what I do – not because I have to do it or am clawing my way out of suffocating debt.

- I am able to do what I love and still spend quality time with the people most important to me – my family.

These experiences have helped me to learn a great deal about myself and the process of true success in life.

I want to emphasize that word "process" because it truly is a process – one that can be made much more simple and fun with the right guidance in place. Someone once told me, "The quickest path to success is directly through the experience of others." I hope that you are able to learn from my story and take away some of my lessons without going through all of the challenges that I did.

I'm a country boy at heart. Always have been, always will be. I grew up on a farm until I was ten years old in Edmonson County, Kentucky. It's the kind of place that you can't even find on a lot of maps so don't even try. This is a place that is so country I'm practically related to all of my neighbors – literally. I grew up with one cousin across the street from me, one next door, and another down the hill.

I had a pretty normal childhood until I was ten when I faced my first big hurdle and my parents split up. I began dividing my time between my parents and between cities – Bowling Green one weekend, Nashville the next, and so on.

You never know the kind of events that will leave a big mark on your life, out of nowhere. A big one came when I was 12 years old and my dad's house burned down. It was one of those unfortunate twists of fate that could happen to any of us – and unfortunately it happened to my family. My dad didn't have the right type of insurance and the family situation quickly took a big financial blow. We went from middle class to... practically nothing.

I found myself spending much more time in a particular part of town where I was a lot more vulnerable to some bad influences around me. It's amazing how much your environment can affect your life, especially as you are growing up. As I will talk about a bit later in the book, I firmly believe that most of us reflect the total sum of the people we spend the most time with. During this period of time, unfortunately, I fell in with some bad influences. I begin getting into petty crime, misbehaving, even dabbling in selling drugs. This is difficult to talk about even today – after all, I know that I have a responsibility to be a role model for my own children. But I think it is very important in life to take responsibility and own your mistakes. And this time in my life was certainly my own biggest mistake.

Taking responsibility doesn't change the truth that we are all products of our environments. If there is easy money to be made in dealing, it can be very difficult to convince a teenager in need of money that it isn't in their best long-term interest. If there seems to be no jobs or opportunities to be found, many in tough areas will gravitate to crime. It doesn't make it right – but it doesn't mean they are crazy either. Not when there is so much more money to be made in dealing than flipping burgers or cutting grass. (This is one reason why we need to show our kids early on just how much opportunity there is in thinking like an entrepreneur and creating opportunities even where none seem to exist.)

A lot of people might tell themselves they will stop at selling weed, but the siren song of more money is hard to resist. I was barely 14 years old when I found myself dealing cocaine as well – heck, I could cook crack in a microwave before I even had my driver's permit.

I was growing up fast and spinning out of control. Robberies, killings – I saw a lot of stuff go down that no kid should. I even had my door kicked in at night by people who knew that I was dealing and had a lot of cash laying around. It was a very scary time.

The big turning point for me came when I was 15 when my good friend Corey was shot and killed. It was a horrific tragedy – one that pains me to think or write about even today. That moment was a wake-up call. I knew that things had to change – or I was bound to end up the same way.

But I could not have turned my life around completely on my own. I believe that we all make our own fates, but we also all face challenges in life that are too big for us to get through on our own. We all need somebody from time to time. And the person who first really helped me turn things around was my Mom.

My mother is truly responsible for everything that I am. I would not be where I am today or have the life that I've been blessed with if it were not for her. She was the one who has always believed in me – not just during the good times when money is rolling in and fun is abundant, but during the tough times as well. She is the one who would pick me up from jail when I had done something stupid, like driving on a suspended license (which I don't recommend you do, especially in the state of Kentucky – a lesson that I learned the hard way). We all need someone in our corner who believes in us, and for me, that will always be her.

Mom was the type of person who would give anything away to anyone. She always thought of everyone else first. It's one reason why today I feel so grateful to get to help take care of her and make her retirement dreams come true.

She had been working with a company called Combined Insurance since I was 12. Incidentally, Combined Insurance was founded by the renowned businessman and philanthropist W. Clemont Stone, whose writings and teachings would later inspire me and have a profound influence on my life. I even had the opportunity to meet him and the great salesman Zig Ziglar. Most kids look up to astronauts or singers – maybe you could tell early on that there was something a bit different about me because I tended to look up to great marketers!

I saw right away what a positive difference her work was making in her life. She was swiftly becoming one of the top sales professionals in the company. But the change I saw in her wasn't just about the work or the money – it was the people and the network that she built around her. Everyone seemed so positive – and they seemed to be doing so well. They began to open my eyes to the idea that there could be a better way for me to use my hustling skills.

I was a born entrepreneur. I was great at sales and loved the thrill of closing a deal. That was what made me good at dealing on the streets. But it was clearly a fast track to nowhere. Sooner or later, I was going to wind up in jail or dead. So what if I took those same skills and applied them elsewhere? To something productive? To something I could feel proud about at the end of the day?

I was "lucky" enough to see enough horrible things happen by the time I was 19 that I decided my ambition was to become a legitimate businessman. I set out to change my life and the lives of others for the better while taking my experiences and sharing them with folks in order to help them get on the fast track to achieving their dreams and ambitions as well. I feel really blessed to be able to turn something positive out of a very dark time in my life – heck, I may not even be a success today if I had not gone through those hard times to begin with.

So I started over as a sales person – only this time, I was selling security systems door to door. I began when I was 18 and knocked on doors until my knuckles bled.

One day a man named Peter Leighton asked her how I was doing. Peter was a Vice President at my mother's company – a big shot. But he still had time to ask my mother about her family and take an active interest in her life away from work. She told him about how I was throwing myself into my new job.

"Why isn't he working for us?" he asked. "He should be selling insurance."

"Well, he's only 18," she replied.

"Let me worry about that," Peter said. When he had an idea, he was the type of person who followed through. And his idea was to give me a shot. Little did I know that he had given me a chance to truly fast track my dream life. Two weeks after my 19th birthday, I was following in my mom's footsteps and entering the world of insurance.

I quickly found that my sales abilities extended to insurance as well. I made the rank of sales manager when I was just eight weeks into the gig, matching a company record that had been gone unchallenged since the 1930s. I was doing well – enough to know that I was done forever with a life selling on the streets. I was going straight and never looking back. Thank God.

I quickly attained the rank of divisional sales manager – and I learned that I had a gift that I would have never guessed. I was a great teacher.

My high school self would have NEVER believed that one. Back then, I was nothing but trouble for most of my teachers! (Needless to say, none of them were sad to see me move on from school either.) But when the subject was something I was passionate about, like sales and marketing, I was able to inspire and educate others. I knew the challenges that they faced and I was able to relate how I had overcome them. It is an unfortunate truth that a great number of people go through life and through their entire professional careers without ever quite finding their unique niche. Studies have routinely shown how the average American is checked out and disengaged on a daily basis at their work. So trust me when I say that I feel very blessed and fortunate to have found exactly what it is that I was placed on this earth to do. I am here to help others fulfill their own potential – specifically through sales and building businesses.

Soon I was spending much more of my time helping to make others into great sales professionals. I became a division sales trainer based out of an office in Dallas. I had the opportunity to travel far and wide in helping to train others learn the same techniques that had helped make me successful – Texas, Oklahoma, Louisiana. I got to see a lot more of the country than I had ever thought possible growing up. I was able to train literally tens of thousands of others in the classroom, helping to give them the skills and mindset to be the best sales professionals they could be.

There were always new challenges to tackle. I had some trainees who were 60 or 70 years old, with more years of experience in sales than I had been alive. But the fact was that times had changed – especially when it came to how to use technology to make sales. Just as I had plenty to learn from them, I had gained enough confidence to know that I had lots of value to teach them as well.

You might think that the rest of my story was a straight glide to success. But we all know that life doesn't usually work that way.

I was on a terrific path for about seven years. The money was good, the experience was great – and then, just as we all experience from time to time, life threw me another curveball. My company went through a corporate restructuring and my position was eliminated – just like that.

It was a tough lesson. I had worked my heart out and truly gone above and beyond in service of the job. But the market is what it is and there are no guarantees when somebody else is signing the front of your paycheck.

Luckily for me, losing my job wasn't the worst thing that I could imagine – heck, it wasn't even the worst thing that I had ever seen. Far from it. The lucky part of going through some times, like I had as a teenager, is that it prepares you for tough times ahead. You learn to roll with the punches and see the potential in any setback.

When I was terminated, I didn't worry too much. After all, I had a beautiful resume. I had trained legions of people to advance their skills. Who wouldn't want to hire someone like me at a six figure salary?

The answer – NOBODY!

One of my big mistakes was that even as I had been earning a great income, I had not been saving or investing nearly enough. It is a common mistake that a lot of us fall into, especially in the network marketing field. We have so much money coming in from all directions that we are just sure that it is going to keep flowing in. So why bother to save? Who needs an IRA? We're young and feel invincible, so it doesn't occur to us to begin saving away for a rainy day. I know guys who went from pulling in six figures a month to going broke. They go buy a new house or a new Benz and the spending catches up to them when things go south.

My own big payday had come to a screeching halt. That's how I went from an annual income of nearly a quarter million dollars to zilch. After all of the success that I had found, it was quite demoralizing to feel like I was starting all over again from the very bottom.

I sent out resume after resume and networked like a mad man. But nothing worked. But I still needed to pay the bills. If I were younger, maybe I would have turned to desperate measures, but I knew that life was behind me now. I would only be doing honest work.

And that's how I found myself, after living a pretty cushy life as a sales trainer, working on a factory floor making industrial batteries. I went from a multiple six-figure a year income to $11 an hour. It now would take me an entire year to earn what I used to bring in each month. The money woes just multiplied from there and I soon found myself in way over my head financially. I even defaulted on the home I was in. You can't live in a house you can't afford and I couldn't make the payments. Soon my car was repossessed and gone as well. Heck, I could not even afford to pay *attention*, let alone pay my bills! My life of luxury was long gone.

The work itself was nothing to write home about. Imagine the lowest form of grunt work that you can visualize – that's what I was doing. There was no heating or cooling, for one thing. If it was 5 degrees below freezing outside, it was 10 degrees below inside. If it was a scorching 100 degrees outside, you better believe it was 120 inside.

It was tough to go from being valued for my expertise in doing something I loved to an entry-level position at best. It was extreme manual labor – don't get me wrong, there is nothing wrong with making an honest living with your hands. I had nothing but respect for my co-workers and everyone else who puts in an honest day's effort. But it was not what I was most talented or capable of doing. I pushed myself, but I knew that I was on a dead end, punching a time clock and working to make someone else rich off of my labor. Something had to change.

I realized that my success really was going to be self-determined. Nobody was going to swoop in and change my life with the offer of a dream job – because, in my opinion, no such thing really exists. A job is inherently something you do to build success and wealth for someone else. For me, if I wanted to fulfill my promise, I needed to think like an entrepreneur. I wanted to fire my boss and stop selling away my life one hour at a time. Nobody ever sat down with me and said, "Here is step one." I had to figure out much of it on my own and by closely studying people I admired from afar.

I went to work building a series of network marketing businesses. There were plenty of hiccups along the way. If you want to read a story of instant overnight success, you are going to have to look elsewhere! Luckily my life had taught me that success is never a straight arrow – there are always setbacks and reversals you have to deal with. I have personally seen it all – going from a luxury condo in downtown Dallas to homeless and back to the beautiful home that I live in today outside Lexington, Kentucky. That awareness that success never comes in a straight and easy line has given me the patience and determination to stick with hustling and building businesses over the long haul.

The great thing about entrepreneurship is that you are never too old or too young to just get started. Like a lot of people, I played it safe at first before I entirely struck out on my own. By now I had two children that I was responsible for and it was on me to provide for them.

So I was still working at the factory even as I was working to set my businesses up. That was a big challenge as I was working 12 – 14 hours a day, 7 days a week. If you are working 4:30 pm to 5:00 am, you don't have a lot of extra time to work with. As a result, I became really effective at time management and maximizing every minute I could find. I would find myself getting in trouble and chewed out because I was always on my phone. My supervisors thought I was goofing off – when in reality, I was busting my ass to set up businesses while still meeting my employee responsibilities. Each day I would have a sales call scheduled for my 30-minute lunch break – sometimes as many as three calls crammed into that brief window of time.

As exciting as entrepreneurship is, it certainly is not for everyone. There are some who are better served by contributing as an employee and having more time to devote to themselves or their families; it is simply a trade-off of what works best for you personally. A good way to test the waters without going "all in" on self-employment is to launch a side business, like I did, while still employed. This can be very demanding on your time, but allows you to see if working for yourself is a viable option – while still keeping the safety net of your job in place before you quit.

I was struck recently by a Census survey that looked at where the average 25 year-old would be in 40 years from now. It found that out of 100 people, their fates differed quite a bit. 36 will be dead; 54 will be broke; 5 will still be working at the age of 65; 4 will be well off and financially secure; and only 1 will be rich.

It makes you think about how your current behavior and routines are affecting your path to your old age. I can assure you that the single person who finished rich and independent had gotten involved in building and running her or his own business. With all of the opportunities on the internet today, there is no shortage of industries to venture into. So when I started out, I was dabbling in a bit of everything – video marketing, energy, and more. I found that even when I was plunging into a completely different market, I would have a lot to learn but the same basic principles of sales and marketing apply across the board. When you look at the world from the perspective of an entrepreneur, you can't help but see opportunities all over the place.

I eventually found an opportunity with a great salesman named Seth Fraser, who helped teach me even more about the art of network marketing. I quickly knew that this was the perfect fit – and my new colleagues knew as well when I rocketed into a spot among the top three income earners in the company. It took about a year, but the month that I finally matched my factory salary from my commissions was the month that I said goodbye to working for someone else forever.

I had picked up a very important lesson from following a buddy of mine into multiple companies. The lesson I learned was to find a company or product that I actually enjoy working with and stick with it. Those who stick and stay are those who get the pay. In retrospect, I should have done that from the get-go instead of getting involved in multiple companies each year. But a big part of life, of course, is learning from your mistakes and taking advantage of them in the future. My advice to anyone would be to find a company or service – or create one yourself, if you can't find one – that you will stay passionate about and that you can have fun with. I have had a lot of financial success in my career, but I am most grateful that I have also been able to have a lot of fun. That is the sort of intangible that does not always appear on a resume or job description but is crucial to your long-time happiness and success.

After a very successful run over the next few years, I finally decided to "retire" from the network marketing profession in 2015 to focus on training and consulting for a number of clients, ranging from Fortune 500 executives to churches and schools. I help my trainees to master sales techniques, ideas, and principles, along with product knowledge. I also run intensive personal self-development courses to help my students elevate their mindsets to perform at a higher level – because success or failure always begins in the mind first and foremost.

I feel blessed that I have had the opportunity to help so many others to fulfill their own potential, helping many of my students to become six-figure earners. It's a lot of money for most people in our country and a difficult income level to hit in many industries. The key is to put your skills and ingenuity to work for YOURSELF, not just pouring your sweat equity into someone else's project.

I can still very vividly remember the feeling of being unemployed. I'm done forever with that. I am now what I like to call "unemployable" – I simply could not abide by someone else's rules and schedules ever again. I like to be in control of how I use my time and I like to be in charge of how fast and big my income rises.

With every experience I've had, I can tell you that I'm still finding out more about my dream-self every single day that I am blessed to live in this beautiful world. There really is no plateau to success or a strong positive mindset, there truly is ALWAYS room for growth. Even when you reach the most grand and lofty version of your dream-self , your ideals of a successful and fulfilling life will continue to evolve and change into something even bigger and more grand! Those who dwell on the past and moan that their best days are behind them very rarely succeed. People who look to the future with optimism and positivity are the ones who make it big.

Originally, I started modeling myself after the sales people and the leaders in personal self-development that my mother put me around when I first got started with Combined Insurance Company. Think of people like Zig Ziglar, W. Clement Stone and the leaders of Combined Insurance. Had it not been for my amazing mother and that dynamic group of people, I don't know if I'd be anything close to the person I am today, and for that I'm eternally grateful.

I didn't realize it while I was doing it, but the whole time that I was making the progressive change from a street kid into a professional salesman and thought leader, I was using the principles and techniques outlined in this book. I didn't know how to be like the guys I saw on television wearing those nice suits and fancy shoes. But I did watch them carefully. I studied their lives and took notes on how they spoke, how they carried themselves. I began modeling myself after them, eventually creating a character based on true stories. I was truly living the stories of the successful people I dreamed to become like.

I know what you may be thinking. "Austin, I'm not in the network marketing game and I don't want to be. I'm not an entrepreneur. What good would your advice be?" Trust me, regardless of what you do or want to be doing, anyone can benefit from these rules and best practices. (I would also push back on the notion that you can't be an entrepreneur, because I believe that we all have entrepreneurial impulses inside, but that is a story for another day.)

I'm looking forward to hearing about the characters YOU design and YOUR journey! I urge you to do me the favor of sharing your stories with me, and when this information begins to change your life before your very eyes, share your journey with me via my contact information that you will find in the back of this book. I may feature your story in a book, blog or publication after I contact you and get permission.

There's nothing that brings me more joy than knowing I helped positively affect someone's life for the better and hopefully you will feel the same.

With that being said…let's begin the journey together!

CHAPTER 1

What in the world do you want? (Do you even know what life you want?)

Everyone who achieved success, and solved each problem as they came. They helped themselves. And they were helped through powers known and unknown to them at the time they set out on their voyage. They keep going regardless of the obstacles they have met.
W. Clemont Stone

Are you living your best life possible? Be honest with me – and with yourself.

Many of us live out our lives and never really develop a clearly detailed picture of our "dream life" and the best version of ourselves we can possibly ever become. We accept "good enough" and we go along with the path of least resistance. Over time we grow so comfortable in the routine and niche that we have carved out for ourselves that we are unwilling to take big chances and shake things up. This is an issue that we intend on addressing in these pages.

How do you expect to get where you are going without the help of a clear picture or a visual map of some sort? It is one thing to set specific goals to achieve but it's another thing to take creative thinking and planning time daily to develop a clear image of what you believe your greatest human potential is…what you could POSSIBLY become, the change you could make in the world, or whatever impact you'd like to make. If you are continually reacting to the demands others ask of you or whatever the urgent crisis of the day is, you simply aren't thinking strategically about the long-term.

There's nothing wrong with writing your goals and objectives down, by the way! I know that if you are a busy leader or entrepreneur, it can be very difficult to find the time to sit down in quiet contemplation. I struggle with it myself – I like to always lean on the side of action. With so much to do, who has time to be journaling and writing deep thoughts all day?

But the reality is that purposeful action stems from careful and deliberative planning. After all, crystal clear visualization is a key to unshakably high belief levels. Without putting a lot of thought into it right now, do you really have a crystal clear image of the character in life that you've become already? Or are you just living unconsciously and going through the motions of your daily routine? Have you been laser focused on developing specific characteristics to become the person you are? Or did you just do your best each day and wind up where you are in life currently by accident?

And let's be honest, did you develop some characteristics that may be a little less than desirable along the way? If so, you should understand most people do at some point and that's okay. But recognizing all of that, there is most certainly something that can be done to propel you down the right path and get you running down that path to your dream life!

Developing a crystal clear and vividly detailed image of your dream-self will give you an increased definiteness of purpose. It will also give you powerful hope, which has been said to be the magic ingredient in motivating yourself and others to succeed! It is also important that we not just think of our dream-self and dream life. You should also make a habit of maintaining a regular journal or at least make and keep notes on what this person we'd like to become is made of. I know that it can be difficult to imagine finding the time in your hectic schedule to add the task of keeping up with a chore like keeping a diary, but it is a very common practice among some of the most busy and accomplished people you can imagine – even several Presidents. If the President of the United States can make time to keep a diary, you can as well. It is all about setting priorities.

To get started, write down what characteristics and mannerisms define the person you envision in your dream life. By picturing these traits and committing them to a written list, you will help lay the foundation for the subsequent steps outlined here in this book.

This is time for a quiet place in which you won't be disturbed and you can actually devote some serious thought. We are about to set the mental and emotional stage for the character that you will be designing and eventually becoming in life. If you've got children, like myself, then maybe even go as far as to lock yourself in a bathroom or your car. I know that it can be difficult to snatch those precious moments of solitude away when you are busy raising a family! I love my two kids more than anything in this world, but they certainly do make it challenging to find quiet time. I ultimately find that time by reminding myself that I want to build a great future for my kids – and that depends on me making time to be my best self and think hard about the goals I have set.

So what are some steps you can take in order to develop this crystal clear image of what it is that you TRULY want to attract in life? How can you get started today?

You really have to know yourself well. Ask yourself the tough questions – including but not limited to the following:

- What job title or position would you like to have?

- What kind of house/car would you like to have? Don't answer in generalities – in vivid detail, go through the interior, exterior – all of it.

- What is your life's mission? (That's a big one obviously and it may evolve over time.)

- If money was no object to you and you could spend your days doing anything that you wanted, what would you do?

- During what activities do you most readily find yourself in a state of "flow," in which you lose all track of time and just focus on *doing?*

- What would you like to be doing that you currently can't because your income or life situation seems to be holding you back? Travel? A new career? A home?

- What kind of spouse would make you happiest?

- What kind of friends would you like to surround yourself with?

- What would your ideal day be like? Not a vacation day or a wedding day, but a typical day in a usual week. (I believe that if you are really free, you don't need to wait around the entire week for Friday or spend months counting down until a vacation.) What would your routine be like and how would you spend your time?

- What kind of positive change do you want to create in the world? What would you want your legacy to be looking back upon your life at the end?

- MOST IMPORTANTLY: How does possessing all of this make you FEEL?

It's very important to be as detailed as possible when answering these questions. It is critical that you attach a feeling of gratitude and love to these thoughts because attaching these positive feelings to the thoughts will help put you in a positive frame of mind. This will develop the kind of attitude and personality that will attract the people and circumstances into your life necessary to manifest this "dream life."

We are really just brainstorming here, collecting detailed thoughts and ideas about our dream-self and dream life. Essentially, we are taking notes on the character we'll be creating and eventually becoming so the drama is in the detail. We need to be able to see the answers to these questions in our mind's eye in vivid detail!

One tip that will help you attach the feelings of love and gratitude to these thoughts is to imagine that you already have these things and you are already living this life, because you WILL be. The higher you place your level of belief and faith in yourself and the process, the easier this will become.

One common practice that has worked well for me is to put visual reminders of my goals in places where I will see them daily. That includes visual reminders of the answers to the questions we just asked ourselves. These will help with one of the following chapters as well. These could be pictures, quotes, affirmations or anything that helps remind you of the task at hand and crystalizes your vision of your dream life. It can be very easy to get focused on the day-to-day grind of life – our commute, getting the kids ready for school, getting our projects at work completed. You can get so wrapped up in just keeping up with the day to day stuff that you TOTALLY lose sight of the bigger picture of what it is that you want to be working toward for yourself. Keeping these visual reminders up where you are guaranteed to see them is a very useful way of nudging yourself and keeping you focused. These cues almost serve as a way of your goals saying, "Hey! Don't forget about me! What are you doing today to make me a reality?"

Create a vision board if you like, but I prefer to incorporate these visual and even auditory reminders into my everyday life so they become an everyday part of my reality. I've even gone as far as to choose ringtones for my phone that might remind me of my dream life. You may laugh, but I actually taped a Mercedes Benz Emblem to my steering wheel for quite a while to help me visualize driving my Benz. Silly, right? Maybe – but I am driving a Benz today. So if you want to have your own pilot's license someday, make sure you have that photo of the plane hanging up right where you can see it!

Part of these reminders may be something that remind you of your life's mission and what kind of character you wish to portray. If they do, that's good! Keeping your life's mission in mind will help you blow past challenges that arise in your life – and after all, everyone has challenges that emerge. It could possibly be a quote or self-message that acts as a conscious reset button to put you back in character and on track to becoming that dream-self. These reset buttons come in handy because we all need constant and consistent reminders to help us get back laser-focused. However you remind yourself, make sure to attach those feelings of love and gratitude and you will find yourself experiencing much better results and enjoying the process even more!

You may feel like you shouldn't be so focused on money or wealth or material objects. There surely is a balance to strike. It's important to not let the pursuit of wealth crowd out the importance of your relationships with friends and family. But it is also key to remember that money itself is not the root of all evil, as is commonly believed – rather it is the love of money. While money is a necessity and a great thing in abundance, I've found that financial success can't be the sole driver of your engine. (And like anything else in life, money will run away from you if you chase it.)

I will say that I've been broke and I've been rich – and let me say that you truly don't know what it's like to just breathe until you have the freedom and peace of mind that comes with not worrying about every last cent.

Think of money as a tool like anything – it can be wasted and abused, or it can help you to build a far richer and more meaningful life for you and your loved ones. It takes money to donate to charity or to invest in businesses or give your kids a quality education, so don't lose sight of all of the positive things that come along with pursuing your wealth. There is nothing wrong about pursuing these goals as long as you do it in the most ethical way possible. As W. Clement Stone put it, "believe that any goal that doesn't violate the laws of God or the rights of your fellow men can be achieved."

Lessons from My Journey

Mentors and role models make all the difference in the world. I want to backtrack to my story briefly to give you an example.

You may remember that during my mid-twenties, I had left corporate America because of company downsizing. It was unfortunate, but that's just part of the corporate America life. After six years of being among the best in the world at what I did, not even being the highest performer or hardest worker was enough for the marketplace. When I put my resume out there in search of a new position, it seemed like there were little to no openings available to pick up where I left off financially. That's when I was forced to settle for that low-paying position in a factory, where I was working harder than I ever had before in my life. I still wasn't anywhere near matching my previous income. It was very dispiriting. I had to produce though – I had a family to provide for and, as you know, bills have to be paid and the kiddos have to eat!

Sometimes, all it takes to completely shift the direction your life takes is one tiny incident or a passing conversation. You might not even know it at the time, but looking back later you will know that it was a turning point for you. I vividly remember one for me in particular – the day a man asked me a question that changed my entire thought process forever. I have never been the same ever since.

I first learned of Kevin while surfing Facebook on the computer in my mother's home. You often hear people say that social media is a waste of time. I think that it is just like anything else in life – it's all how you use it. It can either be a diversion from life or it can be a tool to make your life better. I have been able to use social media as a means of connecting with others to pursue our dreams – and it began with Kevin.

I was on Facebook at that moment because I had plenty of time on my hands – I was broke. I was so broke that as they say, I was actually "B-R-O-K" and the "E" was on layaway. I can laugh about it now, but I was scared as hell back then. I had defaulted on my home, and in need of work. I was even getting my food from the Salvation Army. I was ready to hear a message of hope and optimism about what I could do to turn my situation around. And as the saying goes, you can't possibly say the wrong thing to the right person. That's when I came across Kevin in my newsfeed. And I was the right person for his message. I just hadn't known what I was looking for.

He appeared to be in his twenties, but carried himself with the confidence of an older man, wearing a beautiful suit. His page said that he worked for a health and wellness company called "Diamond Elite." I still didn't know what Kevin did, but I knew what diamonds were – and he looked successful enough to afford them. I didn't care what he was doing – I was excited about it.

I sent him a message and told him that I didn't know what he did exactly, but I wanted to be a part of it. I was that starved to succeed.

Kevin was a master salesman, however. He was quick to use some of the techniques that I would later learn myself. One of the key examples was the habit of "posturing" – carrying himself with the kind of confidence that intrigues people and motivates them to want to learn more. I like to define "posture" as the weakness that others can sense in you or the strength that others sense in you.

Kevin definitely projected a clear aura of strength. So he played it cool when I messaged him. An amateur marketer or sales person might react differently when they have a lead. They might tip their hat about how excited they are to have a potential recruit and jump at any opening they get.

Not Kevin. He coolly responded to my message with a short note, saying that he was a bit too busy right now to help me out. He was out to eat with colleagues. He then sent me on my way to a 10 minute video instead.

Nobody likes a whiff of desperation. People equate being busy with being busy and successful. By sending me to that video, Kevin sent a clear message that he was not hurting for recruits and wasn't dependent on winning me over. It's just as important to remember in sales as it is in dating – that which you chase, will always run away. If you are chasing your prospects, you will likely scare them off because there is nobody who is eager to board a sinking ship.

Not to mention the other thing – this guy was out to eat with colleagues? I could not even afford to buy an appetizer right now. He had friends and money to spare. He sounded like he had the life I wanted for myself.

He had automated his first pitch – if I had turned out to not be interested or too intimidated to follow through, he would not have wasted ten minutes for nothing. (Time is money, after all – and that is true nowhere like in network marketing.)

He was reeling me right in. Hook, line, and sinker! We soon had a meeting set up to learn more. He asked me to meet him at a local Starbucks.

I rolled up right on time – arriving in my banged up 2004 Oldsmobile Alero. Busted tail light. Window wouldn't even roll down, so the car was a complete heat trap during the summer months. I had brought a bottle of water with me; I just simply could not afford to be buying even a bottled water inside the coffee shop. That's how broke I was at the time.

So you can imagine my reaction when Kevin pulled up in a beautiful black Range Rover. At that point, I was ready to do anything that he had said – even if it hadn't been legitimate, I have to admit looking back. I was just hungry to better my situation.

Kevin and his partner Brandon broke down how things worked for me. They explained the network modeling model. It was a revelation to me. It doesn't occur to so many of us that we could go to work for ourselves instead of clocking in and reporting to a manager each day.

I had some concerns though. This sounded risky. What if I couldn't cut it? What about having a safety net if things went wrong?

Kevin didn't blink an eye. He had heard all of these concerns and questions a thousand times. And he had heard a lot of excuses over the years – excuses for why entrepreneurship was too risky. Finally he said to me, "Austin, who do you love more, your boss or your family?"

The question stopped me cold right there in my tracks.

It was confusing to me because of course I love my family more than my boss. I could not fathom why he would ask such a seemingly ridiculous question. I responded by telling him that of course I loved my family more and asked if he was kidding. He then asked "Well, then why do you spend more time at work with your boss than you spend with your family?"

He had a good point. I was working 12 to 14 hours per day, 7 days a week most weeks and barely ever saw my family. Heck, if I DID see them, I was too exhausted to do much and it took everything out of me just to play with the kids for an hour or help out around the house. It wasn't satisfying but I thought it was all I had at the moment.

It was at that time I realized that I wanted – no, I needed – to have true freedom! I needed to have the ability to spend time with my children during the day.I needed the ability to take trips for a week or two at a time without worrying if I would have a job when I got home. I needed to live my life without worrying about someone taking my income away and my family starving! I needed to truly see what the world has to offer me and my loved ones so I needed to find a better way – and needed it as soon as humanly possible because that damn factory was killing me.

I was learning that achieving freedom was all about putting the right systems into place. As I like to say today, the word "system" really stands for "save yourself time, energy, and money." Having a ready-to-go script and a regular schedule in place will allow you to easily duplicate and replicate your efforts on a mass scale and impact far more people than you could otherwise.

He also introduced me to some ways of producing residual income. I was good at following directions and I was hungry for knowledge so I did all sorts of research and training to sculpt my mind into a weapon to relentlessly fight my way out of my situation.

It took some time to get started and it took just about every spare penny that I had to get my first business off the ground. I remember putting an entire paycheck into getting started – that was quite a sacrifice and quite an investment for me. Was I crazy? Was I better off just parking my pennies in a risk-free savings account and spending the next decades of my life working toward retirement? That seemed like the safe pattern that our culture pushes on us. But I knew that I could not wait decades to achieve freedom and independence. The fact is that if you aren't willing to invest hundreds, you are not truly serious about the prospect of making millions.

I'm glad I didn't give into my doubts. It didn't happen as fast as overnight – but it didn't take decades of toil either. I didn't know exactly what I was doing over those first couple of months, but I sure did bring passion to my work. You might say that I was "ignorance on fire." It takes time to develop and build your expertise in any profession. Lawyers and doctors have to go to school and go through apprenticeships for years to master their fields, after all. It is no different in sales – except it can ultimately pay much better and can be a whole lot more fun, in my humble opinion. Within just about seven months, I had matched my full time income with part-time work on a side project which gave me the option to quit my job – and that's just what I did. Man, I'll tell you, I almost wrecked on the way out of that factory as I sped off never to be seen from again! I was hyped!

I started doing EXACTLY what I saw my partner and other successful people in his field do on a daily basis. I began to change my vocabulary to speak like them. I even started to eat differently. After some time had passed, I truly could not quite tell where they ended and I began! I had changed myself to fit in with these guys and be like them because what I had been doing simply was not working and what THEY were doing WAS. They weren't complaining about their problems or kissing up to their bosses or buying lottery tickets in a last-ditch hope to strike it big. They were creating value and building businesses to gain control of their lives instead. I began to look at the world the way they did – through the eyes not of an employee, but of an entrepreneur. It was an amazing lens to put on.

What's the difference you might ask? Well, it isn't simply about money or crunching numbers. Rather it is about looking around you and seeing opportunity everywhere. A lot of us go through life and see things that annoy us in our daily lives. But we often don't do much about them besides grumble and keep moving on. We don't think of ourselves as having the ability to do very much about it. But entrepreneurs see the exact same circumstances and see openings to bring new solutions to life that create value. Entrepreneurs don't just complain about bad taxi cab service or lack of transit options – they create Uber. They don't just whine about overdue movie rental fees – they launch Netflix. They don't look at high hotel prices and just throw their hands up in defeat – they come up with Airbnb. Almost every good or service that you use came to life because an entrepreneur saw a need that wasn't being adequately met and rushed in to fill the void. That spirit of solving problems is just as true whether you are creating a revolutionary new technology app or selling a traditional product like wine.

By devoting considerable time to study these types of people and following in their footsteps, I didn't fit in with the people that were around me much at all anymore – and I didn't care that I didn't. I was happy to stand out. I knew where I was going and the person I was becoming…the life I wanted came along with that. A wise person has said that you tend to become the average of the five best people you spend the most time with. This may be a sobering realization for you. Are you spending the majority of your time with those who are striving for success and encouraging you to pursue the same? Or are you holding yourself back from true growth because of the mindsets of those you associate with? Just remember that if you put a healthy child in a room with a sick child, you're going to very quickly end up with two sick kids. Negativity is just as contagious.

I have realized that I wanted to help as many people as possible to rid themselves of the chains holding them back from living their best life ever. That includes jobs they hate, mental restrictions and negative thought patterns...whatever it may be, I just wanted to help them experience freedom like I knew it. That became my driving passion – really an all-consuming obsession – and by doing so, I was able to move closer toward the life that I desired as well. It might sound like I was being selfish, but the truth is that you can help far more people once you have helped yourself and gotten into a position to succeed. It also gave me more of the life that I want because success breeds success.

By realizing what I wanted my dream-self to be like, my life, over time, became a cycle of riding a wave of constant positive energy. I was receiving more and more resources from the universe to magnify my dream-self more and more! I had consciously designed my dream-self and attracted my dream life.

I think way too many of us spend too much time dwelling on all of the problems and negativity in the world, whether it's in the news or in our finances or in our personal lives. The fact is that there has really never been a better time to be alive and DEFINITELY never a better time to be in business. Just look at all of the opportunities that the internet has opened up to hustle and sell your wares. You never would have been able to access all of these customers and markets in decades past. There truly has never been an easier time in history to become a millionaire (or even a billionaire) so adopt an attitude of openness to all of the opportunities that abound around you. Your reality is determined by your perception – you alone determine what you see and what you focus on. So why focus on pessimism when you can focus on your goals?

How You Can Get Started Today

- **Make a list of the traits that you want to cultivate in yourself.** They don't just have to relate to your work or income – they may also pertain to your relationships or health. You should set goals for yourself in every part of your life, not just work, so that you know what you want to achieve in your home life and for your body as well.

- **Take stock of what is holding you back.** What obstacles or challenges are stopping you from taking action and living the life you have imagined? What can you do to address these obstacles? Are these obstacles really something that you have to be worrying about? Or are they all in your imagination?

- **Make a reminder to yourself.** Put a visual cue of the person you want to be where you can easily see it – not just on a list tucked away somewhere. So if you want to achieve a goal of building a dream home, keep a picture of it at your desk so that it will motivate you to keep striving toward your end goal.

- **Be honest with yourself.** Many of us can fall into the habit of basing our goals or dreams on what others want. Make sure that you truly want whatever it is. Do you really want to be a pro athlete or get into real estate or run for office? Or are you just doing what others have dreamed of and internalizing the plans of others? As a sales representative, I never quite understood the practice of managers setting goals for their teams. To be honest, I firmly believe that you have to be setting goals for *yourself* if you are going to follow through on them.

- **Cut out the negativity.** It is often said that your real character is formed as the net composite of the five people you spend the most time with. So if you are hanging around with a bunch of folks who dwell on the negative all the time – you will too. Associate yourself with positive people and positive vibes.

- **Don't go it alone.** The road to success doesn't need to be a lonely one. Be straightforward with your loved ones, including your friends and family, on your vision for where you want to go. And pick the ones you keep in your life carefully – don't let others stand in the way of your dreams with negativity or doubts.

So who do you want to be? And why haven't you started yet?

CHAPTER 2

Do your research and find your modeling mentors

If I have seen further,
it is by standing on the shoulders of giants.
Isaac Newton

Don't worry too much about being original.

That might not sound intuitive. After all, we hear all the time in the media about the hot new innovation or gadget taking the market by storm. It certainly is exciting to have a great new idea – but having an idea is no guarantee of success. And sometimes looking for one can keep you from taking action. I can't tell you how many promising entrepreneurs or business people I meet who hold themselves back from taking the leap into business because they are still searching for their great idea. My advice to them is to relax a bit with the obsession about being completely original.

The fact is that every great person in history has modeled themselves after another great person – that is nothing new. They've taken certain personality traits, mannerisms, styles of dress, quotes or SOMETHING from multiple people throughout their lifetime and created the person they are today.

Take an example from the world of movies. While Robert De Niro was researching his role for Jimmy Conway in the gangster flick *Goodfellas*, he even went as far as to research how Jimmy held his cigarette. Traits and quirks like these may seem like tiny details, but there is no denying that De Niro was able to summon all of those small touches to create a convincing and unforgettable portrayal of his character. These details helped him sell the role. The power lies in all of these little touches. De Niro's commitment to studying every nuance of the characters he plays is what has made him such an iconic actor – he has played every type of role imaginable, from a lovable grandpa to a washed up boxer. His career is a reminder that all of us can find something to tap into in anyone and we can all try on new personas if we put our minds to it.

As for myself, I take a little something from nearly every successful person I encounter and I make it my own. They don't even have to necessarily be in my industry for me to see something that I want to emulate in my own work. I am not shy about shamelessly stealing from the very best. You know what they say, "There's nothing wrong with being a copycat as long as you copy the right cat!" There truly is nothing new under the sun so don't be ashamed to duplicate models that have worked elsewhere. If it will work for one man, it'll work for another! It's not like you're cursed and it works for Bobby Sue, but won't work for you!

So, in finding the leaders and mentors to take these traits from and model yourself after, use the questions you asked yourself in Chapter 1. Don't set out to emulate just anyone. Set your goals for yourself conceivable, but high. One of my big goals is to expand the number of families that I have helped retire from 370 to 1,000. Is that a big "stretch" goal? Yes. Is it achievable based on my past record and the time that I am willing to invest? Absolutely. It gives me a clear objective to shoot for.

Spend some time thinking hard about the type of life you want to build for yourself and find people who have that lifestyle or those characteristics and make them yours. You more than likely will have to find multiple people – all the better to take the best elements from different figures. You can then begin to study them and model yourself after them. Don't just look at their style or end state – look hard at the traits and habits they possess that you wish to assimilate into your everyday being.

By patching the very best elements of all of these different people together, you will begin to get a better idea on how to become that "dream-self" we have been talking about. It is like a good recipe – you use a dash of Tony Robbins, take a sprinkle of Napoleon Hill and marinate the whole package in some Grant Cardone to give it a little spice! Much like a master chef, you can create something magnificent and new by taking elements from many different sources.

You will find that you have more opportunities to find great mentors if you continue to build your network on an ongoing basis and expand the pool of your professional contacts. I strive to expand my own network of connections by at least five people every day. Some of them may be in person at a conference or a coffee shop; others may be through the internet and social media. Wherever you find them, never settle and never stop opening up your universe up to more possibilities.

You may wish to develop the passion of one leader, the style of dress of another, and the inner circle of friends and associates of another. The important thing is to find them and research them because if it will work for one man or woman, it most certainly will work for another!

You will find that most people are instinctively attracted to those who convey leadership traits. It begins early in school

– some folks are just born to lead and convey a sense of value and direction to others. Leaders can come in all shapes and sizes with all types of personalities, but to truly make it BIG in life – especially in sales and marketing – you need to learn how you can personally convey these qualities and become a leader to others. I call it the "Alpha personality" – a term that can have some negative connotations to some, but it is truly just all about taking the lead. Anyone can attain these traits – it all simply depends on your state of mind.

The difference between an "alpha" and a "beta" is that betas are usually living in a state of reaction. They answer to others. They are slaves to their inboxes and voicemails, letting others determine how they spend their precious time. Everything that goes wrong or poorly is always someone else's fault because someone else is in charge.

An alpha is very different – they take responsibility and chart the course of their own lives. They love and protect the people important to them. They treat themselves with respect and expect it from others. They radiate a sense of positive energy and optimism that others want to be a part of.

The beauty is that you do not have to be born with these attributes. Anyone can learn to be an alpha – and I am blessed that I have had the opportunity to help many do it. I have been blessed in my life to make incredible income doing what I love. I have had the good fortune to take care of my family and travel to places I could have never imagined when I was a young man. But believe me when I say that there truly is nothing more rewarding that can compare with the feeling of helping so many other people to live out their own potential and discover just how much they are capable of.

Remember, however, to never lose sight of who you are at your core. Change up your style and mindset, but don't let go of your inner character. Movies and books are full of stories of those who adopt a whole new persona – just think *The Great Gatsby*, for one example – only to lose touch with themselves in the process of chasing money and external validation. You have to make sure that you are chasing your goals because they are what you want for yourself – not what you think you should be pursuing based on what other people are doing or what other people may think. I have met far too many people in this life who seem to spend all of their precious time cultivating an image or lifestyle to appeal to someone else without ever really considering what they want. If you want a big house or a fast car because that is part of the vision that you have set for your life – great! Go for it! But if you get into the habit of chasing things just because you "think" you should or because you see peers going for them, you may need to rethink what it is you really care about. It's not that money can buy you happiness – it's that it can widen your choices and options that make you happy.

REMEMBER: A short pencil is better than a long memory so take extensive and organized notes while doing your research! You will be using these notes to sketch out a "movie character" in a later chapter. Don't forget to take note of your sources so you can come back to them if need be.

Lessons from My Journey

There was a fellow who reached out to me on a social media site some years ago with some questions regarding training for his direct selling business. It just goes to show how technology can bring people together – if you use it to get ahead and hustle instead of just playing games and goofing off all day.

We began speaking frequently because we got along well and we had a lot of beliefs in common – after all, people typically tend to like people who share a common ground or common beliefs. He had five children and a TON of ambition, plus he was an interesting guy and fun to chat with. My 13 week training program cost thousands of dollars, unfortunately, and he truly had nothing at all left over to invest in it. But for me, I decided that this relationship was about far more than just dollars and cents. I decided that my new friend would also be my new project. From that day on, I began the project of training and mentoring him in what I had learned about business.

Over time, we began talking less and less. I was busy and I figured that he was too. One day I was online and saw a picture of him walking across a stage in a nice suit, accepting an award from the CEO of his company. The video of him achieving such success totally moved me. Apparently, he was doing very well for himself now!

I called up my friend to express my congratulations. I was genuinely happy for him – but I also had a selfish reason to make the call, if you want me to be honest with you. I wanted to learn his secrets for myself. You might say that the teacher had become the student! I asked him, what were some of the keys that got him where he was now? What made the big difference between the man he was and the man he had become? My friend responded by saying: "Austin, you may or may not know this but I have been watching you. Every day, I watch what you say, what you are wearing, how you handle things, the people you surround yourself with, where you go…I have been watching you and I really just started doing what I think you would do.."

This gentleman had transformed his entire existence just by the principles we are going over in this book. It was flattering, but it was also really a heavy moment for me. It just goes to show that you never really know when someone is following you and how much of a difference your actions can make on a person and their livelihood. You could change the world or change a person that ends up changing the world. That man went on to change the lives of literally thousands of people for the better.

The story could very well have turned out differently and he may not have had these successes if he had not slipped into the role of the person he wanted to become like and, most importantly, STAYED COMMITTED to that growth. It is not enough to hit the gym once in a while or kick around some business ideas when you have extra time on your hands. Truly achieving big things requires changing your daily habits and staying focused on your goals over the long haul. It means taking calls and still hustling even on vacation, or even on Christmas morning if necessary. This guy modeled his behavior after what he had seen in me and several others. And by doing so, he unlocked the world-changing human being inside himself.

How You Can Get Started Today

- **Look at people who succeed in your industry**. Study their background, working backwards from where they are today and determine the path they took to get here.

- **Be open minded to successful people in other fields**. Don't limit yourself to emulating only those who are in the same industry or line of work. Creativity is most often sparked by applying ideas and concepts from other disciplines, so seek out examples from unlikely places.

- **Consider also studying those you may not be able to meet**. There is a lot you can learn from books, YouTube videos, and other sources, so don't narrow your sights only to potential mentors and models in your geographic area.

- **Respect the time of your mentors**. If you are lucky enough to arrange a meeting with someone you admire, make sure that you are making the very most of that precious time you have together. Don't just show up and expect to soak in the wisdom – arrive with specific questions and discussion points that you would like to raise. Make sure that the time you spend together is used wisely – there is a very big difference between activity and productivity. Very successful people tend to value their time even more than dollars and cents because they know that is a non-renewable resource. Anyone can add labor hours to make more money, but very high earners focus more on decreasing their labor and extracting as much value as possible from every minute – so make sure they don't regret the time they invest in you.

- **Start a relationship and add value.** Successful people – the kind that you want to emulate and learn from – have generally gotten successful because they are very busy. So make sure that you demonstrate your value to them in providing them updates and how you have applied their guidance. They may be busy, but they will likely find a lot of satisfaction in having impacted your journey in some way.

- **Pay it forward.** Be generous with your time to up-and-comers or those looking to make a transition who come to you for advice as well. Life is a circle and we all owe it to the following generation to pass on our wisdom as well.

So when you hear the word "success," who are the first people that come to mind? And how did they get to where they are today? How did they end up where they are today?

Work hard.
Diversity in different areas.
Talk to people
be interested in other.

CHAPTER 3

VISUALIZE!
Don't think it is, KNOW it is!

Logic will take you from A to B;
imagination will take you everywhere.
Albert Einstein

There are five seconds left on the clock and the crowd is on their feet.

When your favorite basketball player is at the free-throw line and the whole game rests on him making this one shot, what do you think he is doing mentally?

Chances are he's visualizing himself making that shot! He is vividly seeing himself making that basket. He is imagining the sounds of the ball going in the net, the ball gliding off of his finger tips and every mechanism in between all the way up to success on the scoreboard. He is feeling the emotion of the crowd celebrating that he has beat the buzzer and won the game. Elite athletes very typically go through visualization exercises to help them get in the habit of painting a mental picture of what their ideal state of success looks like.

But this strategy is not simply effective for pro athletes alone. You too can develop such a powerful habit of visualization with these steps we're about to go, leaves you hanging. By using them, you can close your eyes and see a vivid picture of the end state you are striving for. You can OWN that life you crave so much!

It is also important you feel you deserve that life you're visualizing, as well. This goes for any profession and attaining any goal. If you are a medical student slogging away toward a degree, you need to be able to vividly imagine yourself in that white coat at the end of the journey that makes all the long nights worth it. If you are an artist, you need to be able to imagine yourself performing in front of a rapt audience. If you want to be an ultra-successful public speaker, you've got to practice writing your speeches and and listening to your voice recordings to see how to make your voice more musical, rhythmic and pleasant. Whatever you are wanting to manifest, you need to show the universe that you are serious about attracting this into your life by the actions you take on a daily basis.

Visualization is an extremely important and VERY powerful practice, if done correctly. You don't need to make it over complicated. Keep it simple; "simple" always duplicates. (Keep in mind that you're reading this from a guy who dropped out of school on his third try at the 9th grade. If I can master this discipline, trust me, ANYONE can.) I call it a "practice" because the art of visualization takes consistent practice to gain mastery. You have to fully commit to visualizing when you do this. The power is in the details of your vision. The realities all great visionaries have created for themselves, no matter who they may be, once started out as just a vision – perhaps one that only they could see. But most folks never develop the visualization habit and therefore they never experience the manifesting power of intense, vivid visualization.

Here's an example from the world of acting. Comedy star Jim Carrey is an avowed believer in the power of visualization. He headed to Los Angeles after high school to break into show business, but quickly found himself broke and struggling for opportunities over the following decade. (Sounds familiar, eh?) One night, overlooking the city from his beaten down car parked in the Hollywood Hills, Carrey wrote himself a check – for $10 million. He dated it for five years later and kept it in his pocket with him wherever he went from then on – including to all of the auditions and casting calls he kept showing up for.

Almost five years later exactly, he landed a $10 million contract for *Dumb and Dumber*. He had driven himself doggedly to achieve that payday for doing what he loved – and it all began with laying out a clear vision of his goal. There are so many examples of other achievers in every field who truly refused to just look out with a negative view like so many around them. They stayed focused on the distant horizon of their goals, no matter how wild or unlikely they seemed to the naysayers. They were able to stay focused on that distant vision because they could see things that the critics in their lives simply could not.

To help give you a better idea, let's do a quick visualization exercise.

Let's focus on your dream car. What kind of car is it? What make and model? What color paint does it have? What color is the interior and is it leather or cloth? How does it smell? What's on the radio, if anything? Is there a CD player or satellite radio? Where are you driving to or are you parked? What are you wearing in this vehicle? Look at the back of your hands…now imagine your hands wrapping around the steering wheel of that vehicle. How does it feel both physically and emotionally?

Now close your eyes and take a second to imagine everything we've just discussed in as vivid of detail as possible and take your time until you feel like you're actually in that car. Focus and visualize every little detail.

When you open your eyes, it should startle you slightly to not be in the car. Once you get REALLY good at visualization, you truly believe for the moment that you are actually IN that reality. You can FEEL it! Over time, you may not even have to close your eyes to get to the state of intense visualization. You will be able to generate intense feelings of gratitude and happiness. You will know the things you're visualizing are right around the corner; they're coming. The beauty of visualization is that it helps makes your goals and the things you are striving for much more tangible. By seeing every inch of the car that you want in vivid detail, you will be able to call back upon those details when you are grinding away to achieve it.

Visualization is an especially impactful tool if you are getting ready for a big event – whether it is a performance or public speaking invitation or big game. Relaxation and deep breathing go along with visualization – these are all tested and proven ways to cope with difficult situations and stay in the moment. When you are getting ready for a big moment, try to picture yourself in your mind's eye as completely calm and confident. Watch yourself performing during past victories with total calmness and confidence. Feel how calm you were in practice or rehearsal the day before, when you were doing the same exact thing you are doing now. You may even wish to have someone film you practice. You can then more readily see yourself as others see you.

The emotions that you cultivate while doing exercises like these help you to develop the personality you'll want and the attraction you'll need to manifest this "dream life," as well. It'll give you hope because you'll be able to actually see that dream life coming into this reality…and honestly, it's a lot of fun too! That's the dirty secret of hard work and success that hardly anyone ever tells you; it is a lot of fun to go out there and achieve your dreams. Way too many people quit before they give their results a chance to catch up with them and before they are able to turn all of that fun into a fortune.

As the great business leader and self-help guru W. Clement Stone once said, "Whatever the mind of a man can conceive and believe, it can achieve." Successful people – I mean REALLY successful people, the ones who dominate the very top of their fields – often get there because they can vvisualize completely new possibilities than everyone else. They don't limit their line of sight to see what they see written in a job description or in their bank account or their resume. They see new businesses and industries and opportunities all around them where nobody else can.

Lessons from My Journey

We all go through a lot of changes as we age and mature. When I was a teenager, I developed some pretty extreme anxiety issues. You might not guess it from the outgoing nature that I have adopted today, but I simply kept to myself. I didn't like going out in public – it made me nervous to be around strangers. I used to make myself sick from worry and I felt hopeless from time to time because I felt like I couldn't control this issue. I didn't necessarily need to leave the house to have an anxiety attack however, I could do that all on my own just sitting alone at the house. What I didn't realize is that the cause of my distress was visualization.

But instead of painting a mental picture of the success that I wanted to achieve, I was practicing negative visualization. I was running vivid pictures of the worst possible circumstances through my head over and over again. It soon became all too easy for me to imagine the worst case scenarios playing out of any given situation. I soon began feeling as if the worst circumstances were actually taking place, even though it was all just a figment of my imagination. I was literally thinking myself into an illness. Now, I wasn't thinking myself into the flu, but I might exhibit all the symptoms of someone with a certain sickness. It was all in my head though! I was visualizing and fearing something that hadn't even happened and may not EVER happen. Doesn't make much sense, does it? Sounds crazy, doesn't it?

It was amazing that by just visualizing these negative thoughts, it could make me feel so strongly. I would make myself feel sick to the point that I was even unable to walk or even talk because I'd shake so badly. It was completely debilitating at times, and it was all from the power of visualization. Looking back, it was pretty incredible that the mind could do that to a fella. It was all due to the lack of direction of thought.

I ended up learning a visualization exercise to do when I began feeling myself drifting into "the dark side" so it didn't end up making me ill. I would try to visualize myself happy and laughing with friends, enjoying myself on the beach. The beach is as close to Heaven as I've ever experienced here on Earth. As many other people have experienced, visualizing the beach is like a breath of fresh air. I would take a few deep breaths and remember that I'm a mind with a body, not the other way around. The mind controls the body and I control my mind. Visualization is incredibly powerful because if you focus hard enough on what you're visualizing, you begin to daydream – and a powerful enough focus on your daydream can mentally take you to the place that you are thinking about.

It even goes for something like writing this book, which was certainly a new endeavor for me. It seemed challenging to condense everything I wanted to say about business and success into a relatively short book. But by visualizing myself typing at the keyboard and visualizing the success of meeting readers in bookstores, I was able to prepare to take on a new challenge as a writer. I needed that vision in order to keep grinding away, just as I needed to visualize wealth and success when I was out there hustling for my first sales into the wee hours of the night.

Pro basketball players and other athletes do it all the time. You might feel a bit crazy at first, but it can make a big difference. At one point I used to even make a practice of writing letters of gratitude to my future self. This came from a tip I learned from the great W. Clemont Stone, who advises people to set aside 45 minutes in your day – no matter who you are or how busy you get – for creative, long-term thinking. The idea is to carve out a bit of headspace from all of the distractions and business to think deeper about the big picture of where you want to go.

That was a difficult idea for me to wrap my head around, as I was someone who preferred to always be in motion. I was often taking and making phone calls from the moment I woke up to the moment I went to bed; I'm holding conference calls, webinars, and Skype sessions around the clock. It can be difficult for me to slow down long enough to really contemplate things. But when I did, I wound up spending the time writing a letter…to myself.

I know what you are thinking and don't worry, I wasn't going crazy! I simply adopted a habit of writing a letter of gratitude to the man that I visualized as my future self. I thanked that person for all of the things that he had done for me and for all of the blessings that I knew I could achieve.

I personally found this to be a very helpful exercise in reminding me of what my goals and aspirations were. Even if I was slammed with work all day long, I would find the time – even if it came late in the middle of the night or in the middle of the day. That time was always valuable – it allowed me to sit and clear my mind, visualizing how I wanted the rest of my day to go.

Over time, I was able to conquer a very strong anxiety issue by practicing these visualization exercises along with breathing exercises. I would visualize how I wanted to feel and then force myself to act that way – and I would even have fun doing so! The emotions aren't subject to reason but they ARE subject to immediate action. That changed my life forever and has worked for others I have shared my techniques with as well. Visualization can become a very powerful tool that you can use to sculpt your character and slip in to the role of your best self – so get out there and use it!

How You Can Get Started Today

- **Set aside time each day for contemplation and quiet thinking.** Make this a major priority on your daily schedule. It may be hard to always find the time with all of the other demands in your day, but you can't let the urgent be the enemy of the important. I have learned time and again in life that I can never put my thoughts on success quite as well as the wise Napoleon Hill. As he once described one of his key principles for success, "Direct your thought, control your emotions and ordain your destiny!"

- **Make a habit of deep breaths.** This is an exercise that you can practice almost anywhere – in traffic, on your walks, wherever. Practicing taking deep breaths gets you into a habit of being centered and focusing on your thoughts.

- **Make your visualizations vivid.** Details make all of the difference in making your visualizations as real and as authentic as possible. So don't just imagine a six-figure income, but visualize how you would use that income to build more security and freedom for your family and yourself.

- **Consider using tools.** You may want to record the vision that you have in mind somewhere you can easily see it. For example, you might try writing the goal you have in mind on an index card that you can carry around with you as a reminder. Wherever you are or whatever you are doing, your goal is right there in your pocket with you.

- **Use affirmations every morning.** Take time to say your vision to yourself – ideally first thing in the morning or last thing at night as a way to center yourself on your primary goals for the day. If you don't have time in the morning or late at night – make time! I've found that you should not wake up each day and plan out your day – you should do that in advance so that you can build quiet time into your schedule for longer-term reflection.

- **Be as specific as possible.** Don't allow there to be any shadows in your vision – clearly state what you are seeking. So don't just imagine wealth, but a specific number and goal that will tell you that you have succeeded in your task. If you've made a dollar, you have made more money than you had before – but that is not a very ambitious goal to be setting when you are capable of generating so much more value. I firmly believe in the saying that "aim for the moon – if you miss, you'll land among the stars."

Are you setting aside time today for some quiet thinking and visualization? If not, what could possibly be more important?

CHAPTER 4

Model, mirror & mimic (If it works for one man, it'll work for another!)

Good artists copy, great artists steal.
Pablo Picasso

A mentor of mine once said "Austin, there's nothing wrong with being a copycat as long as you copy the right cat!"

That quote really stuck with me because he possessed a lot of personality traits and mannerisms I wanted to adopt for myself. I saw them as being useful in my own journey through life. So I took characteristics from my mentor and I still use a number of them to this day. Trust me, it is not stealing – it's paying homage! It may be the way someone talks, a word or phrase they use, or a color they wear frequently. Heck, it may even come down to developing a taste for a specific type of food!

In this chapter, you will be putting the research you've done on the people who possess the traits or lifestyle you are wanting for yourself into practice and incorporating them into your everyday living. You are beginning to ask yourself throughout the day, "How would they handle this situation?" Or maybe you are even asking, "What would THEY wear to an event like this?"

However you are practicing, modeling or mirroring these people, it is very important to be consistent with one or two characteristics that you can focus on until they become habits. At that point, they will eventually become a seamless part of you and your daily routine. Then you may be able to take one or two more characteristics and adopt them into your being.

Modeling another person is sometimes complex but it can also be a lot of fun. Just think of it as an acting or improvisational exercise. It can also be extremely useful because it helps you to detach yourself from otherwise emotional circumstances or situations in your life and ask the key question: "How would my mirror mentor handle this?"

This ability to look at things from an outside perspective is priceless. Yes, of course, it takes practice but as you use it, you will see it pay you dividends beyond imagination!

I have been very fortunate throughout my life to be personally mentored and modeled by some of the very best in the world for our field of network marketing. That includes the people I worked with as well as those whom I have studied on my own through reading, such as Napoleon Hill and W. Clemont Stone. My success didn't come overnight, but from a lot of sleepless nights watching training videos or studying blogs or cracking business books. All of these are crucial parts of learning your craft.

If you are blessed enough to be able to spend time with your mirror mentors in person, take notice of all of the little details. How they might cross their legs, how they hold their pen, how they drink their coffee. Take note of all the little things that make them the person they are. Focusing on these details will help you feel more of a close association with them and the lifestyle they have created. You could ask them simple questions on their opinions and take note of their response. You don't necessarily have to agree with them but this will give you a better understanding of their mindset, which will help you in the next chapter.

Not only do I encourage you to seek out mentors, but I think you also have an obligation to seek out opportunities to serve as a mentor to others. Trust me, you will find few experiences in life to be as fulfilling as helping others to navigate some of the challenges that you have faced yourself. I have found that when you help others for a living, you will find that you never have a shortage of friends. I have heard it said that a millionaire in network marketing is someone who has a million friends. And that is certainly true in a number of different fields as well. People are always asking me why I work so hard, but it honestly doesn't feel like work when you have the opportunity to interact with so many wonderful people and leave an impact on their lives. I would do my work even if I didn't get paid for it.

I have seen an unfortunate trend in which many people simply seem to forget where they have come from when they succeed and lose all interest in paying the good deed forward to someone else. You owe it to others to spread your knowledge and experience to those who want to follow in your footsteps as well. Today I am about as busy as I can possibly imagine between all of my business holdings and being the best father possible to my children – heck, even as I am writing this, I can see my phone buzzing with the latest request for business! (Not the worst distraction to have.) But even with all of these competing demands on my time, I still always make time to provide counseling and mentoring to others. If you show me your schedule, I will show you what you value – there is always something urgent and important to be done, so if you truly care about mentorship then you need to *invest* in that time as a priority.

Lessons from My Journey

The #1 sales manager for a Fortune 500 company I worked with was a fellow named Rob. Great guy! Rob could go out and produce a normal person's full week's production in a single day and he had a blast doing so! I never knew how one man could out-perform my entire week's production in a single day. I wanted to be the best that I could possibly be, so I asked him if I could ride along with him on a day's work just to observe him in action. I asked if I could take notes and watch him and how he was able to produce such incredible results. Thankfully, he agreed. I was super excited and had my pen ready to go!

I studied Rob's mannerisms, his voice inflections, the words he used that prospects responded well to. I studied how he dressed, how he introduced himself…heck, in all practical aspects, I was ready to become this man if it meant my success! If he did as much as just cross his legs, I did. If he held his pin a certain way, so did I. I truly was his mirror reflection for all intents and purposes.

I studied Rob every day for a full week. At times it almost felt like I was on the verge of practically being a stalker! You may feel this way a bit sometimes when you are studying the mentors you have identified. I then went out on my own to apply the lessons I had learned from this incredible leader.

Well, you will never guess what happened…my results copied his as well. My sales multiplied by four times just during the first week on my own alone. Things continued to get better and better as time went on with no end to success in sight. I practiced what I had learned more and more. It became easy! And I owed all of my success to my ability to slip into the character of Rob. I had proven that acting can create real world results.

I had the chance to mirror him in person, to take notes on his actions and behavior so I could model him later. I had essentially created a "Rob" alter-ego and slipped into that role to boost my sales exponentially. I was able to do things that I would have been much more nervous about if I had been thinking of myself as "Austin" the whole time. It truly is amazing what a big difference it can make for you to make that mental shift to a new persona. This is a strategy that I have continued to employ throughout my career.

I did essentially the same thing with my mentor John Whitaker, during my time with Combined Insurance Company.

John had some very thick skin – which is an invaluable skill if you want to succeed in sales, by the way. He would not let anything upset him or ruin his day. He also always maintained a great sense of humor – which I have tried to always maintain as well. Life is just too short to not be having any fun!

Like most things in life, this technique has now come full circle. When I began my career, I was looking for others to model – and now I am humbled today to have others coming to me for advice. I have encountered several people throughout my career who have told me they mirrored me or learned things from how I did something and it worked well for them.

Remember: If it works for one person, it will work for another! That's why you never should be too stubborn to try modeling your behavior after someone else. Why reinvent the wheel when others can show you the tools for success that have already been proven to work? It is far more efficient to build off of the results that somebody else has found and to try to improve on their model rather than to begin from scratch.

How You Can Get Started Today

- **Get up close and personal.** Of course some figures that you admire will be impossible to meet, but try to meet some that may be within reach. Just having the chance to have a coffee or conversation can give you better insight into how they think and organize their success strategies. There is nothing quite like the chance to ask those you respect questions in real time.

- **Keep practicing.** It may not feel comfortable to slip on someone else's persona right away, so keep at it and don't give up. It takes some time to break the habits and unconscious routines that you have set for yourself, so take your new "performance" one day at a time.

- **Keep things in perspective.** You can't expect yourself to be a world-class performer or as accomplished as the person you are modeling yourself after – at least not right away. So keep in mind that you are just borrowing a few ideas and tricks, not expecting yourself to change overnight.

- **Keep your creativity hat on.** Your mentor or role model may have not encountered the same exact challenge that you are facing, but you can still use their example. Think about how they might tackle the same obstacle if they were in your shoes

- **Sort out the good from the bad.** Respecting someone doesn't mean that you have to put them on a pedestal. Figure out what traits or behaviors your role model exemplifies that are not helpful as well. The beauty of following in someone else's footsteps is that you can ideally avoid many of the pitfalls and mistakes that they have made along the way of their own journey.

- **Stay open minded**. You don't have to model the behavior of someone who looks like you or comes from a similar type of background that you are familiar with. The beauty of acting, of course, is that you can be anybody that you want. You may find that you have much more to learn from someone of a completely alien walk of life.

Today is your fresh opportunity for a new start. Why don't you get out there and try walking in someone else's shoes, looking at the world from their perspective? You may be surprised at what you see.

CHAPTER 5

Create your character!
(Slip into your role)

Patience, persistence and perspiration make an
unbeatable combination for success.
Napoleon Hill

I'm ready for my close-up, Mr. Deville! This is where it gets REALLY fun!

We have already spent some time thinking of ourselves as actors in order to achieve success. Let's switch up gears now and put ourselves in the shoes of another key player in the movie industry – the screenwriter.

I want you to think of yourself as a scribe who has set out to design a character based off all of the information that you have gathered about your mirror mentors. Closely examine all of the traits you've written down that you wish to possess. I hope that you have been taking good notes! You are going to use this information to design the look, the sound, the attitude, the atmosphere and the entire being of this character so that you can slip into this role to attract your dream life! Not only is this part a lot of fun but this is really where you start to see a lot of results come your way quicker and quicker!

Ask yourself some of these key questions while you are designing the role that you want to assume for yourself:

- How do they dress? Do they dress casually or do they prefer more business-like attire?

- How might they smell? Cologne, soap, body wash or other scents can leave a lasting impression!

- What is their facial expressions for different situations?

- Do they have any verbal tics or favorite phrases that they often trot out?

- What is their daily routine like? When do they wake up, when do they exercise, when are they at their highest energy levels?

- What are their political views, if any?

- What kind of goals do THEY have for themselves?

- What kind of people do they surround themselves with? Don't be hesitant to reach out to people outside your circle from time to time and seek out alternative viewpoints. You may likely find that even many of the most affluent members of society can be more inviting than you might imagine.

- What is your character's mission in life? This answer should be especially detailed.

Now that you have recorded all of this data, use all of this information and write out a description, possibly even a visual sketch of your character. Remember, you are the screenwriter so you are in the driver's seat. It is your concept of a world that you are building. You have the power to put words into characters' mouths and decide their fate. It is your responsibility to breathe life into this character and the details matter. You will also want to make sure you have a general guideline to go by so you can begin immediately on slipping into this role which is your dream person.

We are going to have some fun with this! Don't get caught up in designing every little characteristic so much that you wait until it is a full character before you get started. Sometimes you have to get started even before you are fully ready. You truly have to learn to fly the plane while you are already in the cockpit! You can take one or two characteristics at a time and start assimilating those if that helps you get started but the most important thing is to GET STARTED.

This is a good rule of thumb in general, to tell you the truth. Far too many would-be entrepreneurs and strivers seem to prefer to wait until the perfect moment to get started on launching their projects; but fortune will also smile on the one who just gets moving and learns along the way. Planning and mapping out your vision are invaluable tasks, but don't let them stand in the way of simply getting moving. Life is too short to just sit around and plan forever. I PROMISE that your life is going to fly by much faster than you can even imagine – that's something that anyone who is a parent knows all too well. Why not make the most of the time you have here? So plan your work, but also work your plan.

Everyone is different and you will obviously have your own unique traits that you want to see in your character. But some common ones that tend to come up for many entrepreneurs are confidence, charisma, and courage. It surely takes all of these elements to some degree in order to build a great business and maximize your potential. You may feel as though you are someone who lacks these traits, but applying what your mentors have done should give you the ability to pretend if you have to! You might be amazed at how many really successful people say that they suffer from "imposter syndrome" – they don't really feel like they are talented either. They feel like everyone is going to catch on to them eventually. It is a very common feeling, so you are in excellent company!

People around you will certainly notice a difference in you. They may even feel threatened a bit by the actions that you are taking to move to a new level and change your life situation. This can be challenging, especially when you are hearing resistance from people who may be very important to you. I just encourage you to remember that one of the most important things is to have love in your heart for all and an intense PASSION in the way you move and do things. In time, the people who really support you will understand.

The folks around you and the people you meet will see that you're moving toward this "dream life" with or without them. Beware, because once you start to do better and become more, it is very possible you could receive some criticism and negativity. That's more than fine – it is inevitable that when you achieve something big, you are going to upset some folks along the way and invite some criticism.

You will also start to attract a different kind of person into your life as well because you'll start to do things as you have always wanted. You will put yourself in the location of different crowds and become attractive to a different group. This can truly be a blessing and it may open some surprising doors so be ready when opportunity presents itself. If done correctly, you will literally begin to attract your dream life! You would be amazed at the impact it can have on your motivation just to associate with others who are just as motivated as you to make the most of their potential.

Do you want to have some fun with this step? Dress up as your new character and plan a day to begin living as this person so you can go out and make a day of it…heck, you can even make a full weekend of it! Have fun with this step because eventually, you will end up becoming a version of this person. I say that term "a version" because as you start to progress toward what you currently believe is your dream person, your thoughts and views might change slightly. You may find yourself in the strange position of "losing yourself" somewhat. Or it is quite possible they you could change dramatically!

Now don't confuse this with being "fake." The whole point of this book is to help you realize the person you COULD be if you set out deliberately with a plan to become the absolute best person you could possibly be and make the full use of your potential. Make it a point to set out a plan for yourself and follow through on the commitments you have made to yourself. It is absolutely instrumental to have a vision of where you want to go – as the Bible tells us, "Where there is no vision, the people perish."

You need to realize that the person you envision initially may evolve as you complete the steps outlined in Acting Classes because YOU will evolve. Success is an ever moving target. The journey takes time. And trust me when I say from my own experience that personal and professional growth can give you different outlooks on what is important and valuable.

Lessons from My Journey

I was once watching a video of one of my first real mentors, W. Clement Stone. I realized that I wanted to adopt a persona similar to his, which almost seemed to project an air of mystery. He played his cards close to his chest and left you wanting to know more. I also wanted to channel his ability to be able to help people and give to others. Mr. Stone donated over $600 million of his own money to different charities during his lifetime and helped countless people achieve their dreams, myself included. I definitely wanted to do that!

But I had other models too. In watching a gentlemen named Steve from another company, I realized that I wanted to emulate his style of dress. This man was SHARP and always looked like a million bucks!

By looking at a number of individuals whom I admired, my true self began to come into clear focus. I began to piece together who I wanted to become by watching how Tony Robbins spoke; by how my mother built rapport with folks so well; by how my district manager, John Whitaker, always joked around and made a point of having a fun time no matter if he was working or off the job. Like the old blankets my grandmother made out of patches that she accumulated over the years she lived, I pieced together over time who I am today from a slew of people. Most of them never knew that I was watching or studying them. Even today, I find things people do or ways people handle certain situations and make a mental note for myself to incorporate them into my own being.

Just between you and me, I will let you in on a little secret. I also have a slight fear of speaking in front of groups, but it is an unavoidable part of what I do in life. You may not even know it from seeing me speak, but it is something that I have learned to manage over time. You learn to get used to being out of your comfort zone and fake confidence, even when you are rattled with nerves. Even today as I take the stage for an event, I still feel some butterflies.

My heart thumps in my chest, I forget what I am supposed to say and I start to sweat – but I refuse to let any of that stop me. I simply refuse to let it stop me from getting up there on stage because it has to be done. It has become part of my character and something I have to do to be the person I want to be. So sometimes, I slip into the role of one of my own personal favorite characters – Tony Stark from the *Iron Man* movies. Going back to some of our visualization exercises, I literally visualize myself suited up as a superhero before I step on stage. I enjoy the way he handles himself when addressing groups and it helps me detach myself from the fear I am feeling… but shhhhhhh. Don't tell anyone. This will be our little secret!

How You Can Get Started Today

- **Don't label yourself.** If you are going to assume a new role or character, you can't limit yourself based on how you have thought of yourself in the past. So don't hold back from opportunities because, "I am not a social person," or "I'm not the type of person who goes to events like this," or "I am not creative."

- **Embrace a growth mindset.** Be willing to change and adapt. This may mean venturing away from your comfort zone, as that is where all growth and evolution happens.

- **Say goodbye to negativity to create the best performance.** The only person who can talk you out of becoming a new person is you. The average person has thousands of negative thoughts in any given day – they are often reflexive habits. Don't pay them more attention than these thoughts deserve. The important thing is to not give into negative and destructive thinking.

- **Practice and rehearse everywhere you go.** As the Bard wrote, all the world is a stage. Use all of the ordinary moments throughout your daily life – from your commute to your grocery shopping – as opportunities to try on the persona of your new role that you are crafting for yourself.

- **Let go of embarrassment.** The fear of looking like a fool can be fatal – it holds back many of us from taking chances and risks. If you are overtly worried about what others will make of you, you likely won't be able to fully step into the new role.

- **Be open to experimenting.** You can mix and match roles and take chances that you would not take in your normal mode of behavior. Strike the words "I don't do that," or "that's not me," from your vocabulary. Leave all possibilities on the table.

What are you doing to cultivate your new character today? How do you feel in this role?

CHAPTER 6

Fail to succeed!
(Begin your transition with the knowledge that success is often a series of corrected failures)

I have not failed.
I've just found 10,000 ways that won't work.
Thomas Edison

I know that I have talked a lot in this book about my successes. I am proud of them. But don't get the wrong idea – the road to success has been a long and winding path, not an easy glide. I truly can't tell you the number of times I have failed, sometimes dramatically, before I had any success in some of my endeavors. Just how many failures are we talking about here? Well…is a bigillion an actual number? What comes after infinity?

I truly cannot even count high enough to give you an accurate estimate of how many times my ideas have crashed and burned despite my best intentions and efforts. Heck, I am still failing at some things that I am trying to accomplish. That includes the realm beyond just professional endeavors, to include tasks like understanding how to be the "perfect" parent or understanding the female mind. (I may be working on that last one for the duration of my natural life.)

I try to keep in mind that failure is a prerequisite for any kind of success. Colonel Sanders failed over a thousand times at selling his secret recipe for fried chicken and that stuff is pretty darn good! (After all, I am a Kentucky boy all the way through. Always have been, always will be.) You have to realize that in many instances, success is just a series of corrected failures. There will almost inevitably be many obstacles to overcome when trying to do anything substantial with the life that you have been given. I believe that when the Devil sees you trying to make a life-changing move, he throws even more obstacles in your way. But often, you will hardly notice many of those so-called obstacles if you're laser focused on your goals and the desired outcome.

Another benefit of failure is that it has a way of weeding out all of those who aren't really committed to following through on their visions. How you respond to adversity and setbacks is one of the key determining factors in who succeeds and who flounders.

I have heard time and again from extremely successful people (and learned for myself) that the secret to success is setting goals – and a key to achieving any big goal is knowing exactly where you're going. (As Lewis Carroll famously put it in *Alice in Wonderland*, "if you don't know where you are going, any road will get you there.") By generating a visualization of the end result, you have an image of the motivation that you need to push through all the obstacles. It's all about KNOWING the outcome will be what you wish because you are going to make it happen! You need a champion level intensity on a daily basis because, if you've followed the simple steps outlined in this book, then you know who you want to become. You know what your dream life looks like and you now have the mechanism to become that person and enjoy your life to the fullest.

One other huge tip to overcoming these obstacles and staying laser-focused is to know WHY you are doing what you're doing. Make sure that you have a strong enough reason to motivate you – a motivation that not only will stay at the forefront of your thoughts, but also at the forefront of your heart.

It might feel selfish to be so focused on bettering yourself, but I think your goal should be selfish to an extent. You absolutely have to tie in a very strong emotion with your reason for doing something substantial. For me, I can very vividly imagine what it was like to be broke and I am terrified of ever going back. That keeps me hungry and still motivated – because there is no way I will ever be broke again.

So many of us spend our daily lives just walking through the motions because we haven't factored in the emotions that should be driving us. By getting our hearts involved, our goal becomes a white hot burning desire. You know for sure that your "why" is strong enough when you begin to lose sleep over it consistently and when you think hard enough about it, you start to tear up or get your blood boiling. Once again, it all comes back to visualization and knowing the details.

For the most part, life is about quality AND quantity – experiencing as much as the world has to offer and making the most of it while also remembering to help others and take their success as seriously as your own. Zig Ziglar said it best: "You can have everything YOU want if you help enough people get the things THEY want!" Even the Bible clearly says that service to others is the path to greatness! It's like I like to say – service before self; with that, success takes care of itself.

When you find yourself in the position of "failing" or encountering obstacles, try to always take a step back and ask yourself a few key questions that can help you get back on track to making progress.

1. What can I learn from this?

There is always a lesson to learn and we grow in value as a person with each lesson. My heroes W. Clement Stone and Napoleon Hill advise us to search for the seed of equal or greater benefit in every challenge or adversity, and there always is that seed in every situation. That seed of benefit will always be there for the person who's looking for it with the right attitude. Learn from each and every adversity so it becomes a character building step on your ladder to success!

2. What's great about this problem?

When confronted with a problem, don't just dwell on the negative. Anyone can do that. If you look closer and keep an open mind, you may find that your challenge holds the potential to help you gain in knowledge or skills or perspective. When you come through on the other side, you may well find that you are stronger as well as more prepared – and others can also gain from the wisdom you have created when you grow from overcoming that challenge. Having issues and stepping up to overcome them makes you a more valuable leader in life. The experience you gain when overcoming obstacles is truly priceless.

In theory, we should never struggle with the same issue multiple times if we learn from them. However, we know this may not always be the case, but we can certainly be prepared if and when said issue should arise again. This also helps us become better mentors because of that added value of the experience and the empathy we can gain for others going through the same issues.

3. What is NOT perfect YET?

A big part of the personal self-development process is finding out what areas of your performance or approach are in need of improvement. As we're going through our success journey and slipping into the role of the character that we have created in the previous chapters, we fine tune our character, our surroundings, our mindset and our life. Keep in mind that success is a moving target and there is always room for improvement. Don't get caught up in trying to be "perfect" though, because perfection isn't for us humans. (Certainly not for me!) We can certainly get closer to perfection by asking what's not perfect about the situation we are failing at and then taking action to correct it or make it better.

4. What am I willing to do to make it the way I want it? What am I willing not to do?

Sometimes, you've got to be willing to either give up a habit or a vice. Or maybe you figure out that you have to add a safe guard. Maybe you need to add a good proactive measure to your systems while performing a certain action or task so you don't create more challenges.

Maybe you realize that you have got to stretch a little before you take off running! Maybe you need to find one new thing you love about your significant other each day to work up the courage to propose. Maybe there is just one little thing or a new series of things you need to do each day to keep you from failing or get you closer to your goal.

What are you willing to do? What are you willing to give up or to not do?

5. How can I enjoy the process?

Often, the answer to this question is a simple word – faith.

I don't just mean having faith in something spiritual, but having faith in yourself and what you can achieve. Having faith in your ability to grow into an even better and more effective person will help give you sustenance for the tough times. Overcoming challenges and assessing how you could do better next time will make you a more effective leader – one who is capable or smiling even through challenges. After all, it can't rain all the time and an effective and focused person remembers that "this too shall pass." Life is too short to spend it upset or in misery. You have got to find ways to enjoy the process and realize that no matter what's going on at the moment, it is helping you get to where you want to be in some way. Even if you can't see how it's helping you quite yet, you will find the experience invaluable in the long run.

Another important thing to know is that fun is much like a magnet that attracts success. We all like to be around people who make us feel good and part of something exciting. Having a dour mood isn't just bad for making friends, it is bad for business too. It has never been advantageous to be negative or sour, so make the deliberate decision to not cultivate a bad mad. You know there will be challenges and tough times along the way – but you can still decide that no matter what, you're going to have fun and enjoy the process like a rock star!

If you adopt the habit of approaching challenges with a focused winner's mindset, you will realize this is just one more step toward your dream life! If you love what you do, it won't even feel like work. That's how I'm able to keep grinding it out when everyone else is taking a break or enjoying a holiday. While they are taking those extended breaks, I am still going at it. If you truly love what you do, the work itself will rejuvenate you.

Lessons from My Journey

Before I started working full-time for myself, I used to run a sales training class. I found it very rewarding to help pass on my knowledge and what I had learned to others. I had a student who seemed to have quite a bit of trouble retaining information. She didn't do well on the tests, she seemed nervous when I called on her, and she lacked confidence in what we were doing in class. When I would turn to her to answer a question in front of her fellow classmates, she would invariably freeze up and nearly start crying. She was so afraid, she was paralyzed! I would call on her and she would get the answer wrong and that was only if she tried.

On the second week of sales training, I called on her to answer a question that I knew for certain she knew the answer to. I had taught the class a simple formula to help them with their sales approach that I called "RRAA" – that stood for "Relax, Relate, Assimilate, Action." It's very simple, but I have found it to be a very helpful device to keep in mind when I am nervous or approaching a difficult situation. The phrase acts as a trigger to tap into the most confident, capable version of self.

She instead responded, "I don't know. I have no idea!"

I was beyond frustrated. I just knew that she was capable of so much more. I knew for certain that she knew the answer. In this class of about 30 of her peers, I told her that we were not moving on until she got the answer. She kept saying that she didn't know. I knew that I was really putting her on the spot in a moment when she was fearing the judgement of her classmates. But success in every endeavor often requires that you take the leap of faith and step out of your comfort zone. Finally I told her to tell me what she DID know – and just try.

Wouldn't you know it? She responded with the PERFECT answer to the question I was asking…the absolute best answer she could have possibly given: "Relax, Relate, Assimilate, Action!"

I had known all along that she knew the answer. I later gave her a little private coaching on how to fail her way to success. The important thing, I told her, is to smile and enjoy the process. After that, she did not seem to have so much of an issue in class any more.

Even after she got out into the field and started selling, we kept in contact. She struggled at first and every time I talked to her, she still seemed a bit discouraged. I made a point of reminding her of the instance when she failed her way to successfully answering the questions in class.

This young lady went on to become an executive for a Fortune 500 company and she is continuing to climb the ranks of her profession today. She is just killing it! If you saw how poised and confident in her abilities that she is today, you could never have imagined that she was once a student too shy to speak up in class and answer a question that she clearly knew the answer to. She now tells the story of how she failed her way to success each time she is asked to speak to a group – groups much larger than the classroom that she had been so nervous to speak in front of. Think for a second about the fact she used to almost cry when asked to answer a question in front of a class of only about 30 or so people – and now she is speaking to groups of hundreds of people at a time.

She earned that success herself. But I still must admit, it fills me with a lot of pride knowing that I was able to play some small role in helping her to fully use her talents and abilities.

She explains that it is not about how many times you get knocked down that counts, but how many times you get back up and start swinging again! She also explains that sometimes people just don't have enough faith in themselves and what they're capable of. All too many times, many of us mentally give up long before we even give ourselves a chance. She explains that she used to be guilty of this – but now she has developed a sense of patience and confidence. It took her time, but she has come a long way. Kudos to her – she found a way to enjoy the process.

Each and every one of us face our own challenges. It is not the problems in our lives that define us, but our attitude toward them. How we handle obstacles reveals our character and helps us become the people we are striving to be. Expect challenges and embrace them as one more step toward the realization of the dream character you've created.

How You Can Get Started Today

- **Embrace your past failures.** If you are anything like me, you most likely don't really enjoy dwelling on the times you have fallen short of a goal. I get it – I'm a future-oriented person too. But it's important to reflect on missed opportunities to determine what to change next time.

- **Embrace risk.** Nobody ever achieved anything great in this world without being willing to fall flat on their face and make a fool of themselves. Adopt an attitude that leans into being okay with taking calculated chances.

- **Take the long view.** Remember that no setback is permanent and any failure is a chance to learn something that will help you next time. Most problems don't look nearly as bad looking back years later – or even after a good night's rest.

- **Diversify your chances.** Simple math holds that if you increase your opportunities (and your income streams) you increase your odds of success – as well as your odds of failure. People who fail a lot aren't necessarily untalented – they simply take more chances than the average person. So give yourself more chances to make your mark. I was once standing in the garage of a friend of mine who had made millions in the network marketing business. Surrounded by all of the beautiful cars he had been able to buy for himself, I asked him the secret of his success. He simply shrugged and said, "Everything works a little." That's why you need to invest in multiple income streams and multiple platforms for reaching potential customers.

- **Be easy on yourself.** Don't take your failures personally or berate yourself – you need to think positively in order to make the most of your setbacks.

- **Learn from the failures of others.** Take heart in the stories of all of those who have come before you and managed to bounce back from major failures – trust me, there are plenty of examples. (Hint – I am one of them!)

What have been your biggest failures? And what did you learn from them?

CHAPTER 7

Dare to succeed – a few closing thoughts

I challenge you to make your life a masterpiece. I
challenge you to join the ranks of those people who live
what they teach, who walk their talk.
Tony Robbins

We have been on quite a journey together over the course of this book, haven't we? By now, I imagine that you are probably "getting it."

You may be understanding by now that acting classes are not just for performing. They are a crucial part of creating the person that you want to be. Designing a character forces you to apply universal law, often referred to as the law of attraction. Of course, we are creating our lives and circumstances by our thoughts, either consciously, subconsciously or unconsciously. We can potentially change everything at the drop of a dime if we truly make up our minds and our hearts to do so. However, it typically takes some time to develop a different mindset and thought pattern. So have fun along the way – make it a priority to cultivate faith and enjoy the journey.

Life truly IS what you make it – literally, by what we tell ourselves on a consistent, daily basis and how we view our challenges and gifts. Use self-affirmations and self-motivators to help keep you going through the tough times. I like to keep written adages in sight when I wake up each day that inspire me – mantras like, "Success is achieved by those who try and keep trying with the right mindset!" Or "Where there's nothing to lose and a great deal to gain if successful, by all means, try!"

There was a time in my life when I would make excuses about why I was late or broke or unhappy. Fortunately I quickly learned that nobody else was impressed by how good my excuses were…and I sure could not pay any of my bills with an excuse. You can make excuses, or you can make progress. Happiness and satisfaction begins with taking responsibility for your life. Taking ownership of your decisions is a key part of truly growing up. Instead of using the words coming out of your mouth to complain about your situation, why not use them to reach customers and *change* your situation?

You will notice that the successful people you want to emulate spend very little on excuses or blame. They keep their head down and keep plowing forward on work. They don't run around telling everyone about the vacation they want to go on or the fitness level they want to reach or the book they want to write – they cut out all the excuses and focus on getting it done.

You can't let setbacks in life skew your perception of what you are worth. I was talking with a friend recently who was lamenting how broke he was. His bank account was over drafted. I warned him to not confuse his self-worth with the worth of his bank account. Somebody out there is always out there getting it done with less resources than you. They have more excuses they could be using, but instead they are out there just *killing it*. I've seen guys who were homeless start out in network marketing and hustles. It doesn't take any special talent or special advantage to put in effort, cultivate a work habit, and show up to opportunities on time.

I encourage you to spend some time reflecting on what the character you have designed would do in certain situations and circumstances – and then act on that immediately. Make it a priority to help others with their issues and focus on your character and the role you have committed to slipping into… your best self!

If you find yourself drifting along or in need of direction, refer back to the notes that you have taken on the people you admire or the character you've created. If you absolutely need to, start the process over from ground zero! One important thing to realize is that as long as you're actually trying to make some sort of progress in the right direction every day, you are doing much better and doing more than most people out there. It is all about consistency and belief.

You truly can begin to dress like, act like, think like and become the very best version of yourself. You can create a dream life that will surpass all former ideas of what you thought possible if you use the principles outlined in this book daily. It is crucial that you take stock of the fact that your time on this planet is limited. It may not feel that way when you are younger, but we are all living on borrowed time. All that you can control is the effort you invest into building your life and the relationships you build with others. As W. Clemont Stone puts it, "Success is not for the chosen few. It's for the few who choose it."

At this point in my life, I'm blessed to be able to take the long view. All I want to do is be the best parent possible and do my small part to leave a better world for them and for their children. Believe that YOU too can affect the world and all those around you on a global scale, if you truly decide to do so. The limits are YOURS to set, not anybody else's…so enjoy the journey and follow through. This life you have created is yours – so make it your very best.